HOLLYWOOD GOES ON

HOLLYWOOD GOES ON LOCATION

By Leon Smith

POMEGRANATE PRESS LTD. LOS ANGELES • LONDON

This is a Pomegranate Press, Ltd. Book

Published By Pomegranate Press, Ltd.
Text copyright © 1988 by Leon Smith
All contemporary photographs are by the author unless otherwise credited.
Photographs copyright © 1982, 1984, 1988 by Leon Smith.
First Printing 1988

The Library of Congress Catalog Card Number is 88-610612
ISBN 0-938817-07-8

A Note on the composition:
Cover Design: Tony Gleeson
Book Design: Ben Martin
Xerox Ventura Publisher® Consultant: Leroy Chen
Editorial Assistant: Kathleen Resch
Cover photograph hand-tinted by: Jean Pritchard

Typesetting and page formatting by computer using
Xerox Ventura Publisher® and Microsoft Word® software
output through a NEC LC890 Postscript® PagePrinter.
Body type set in ITC Bookman.
Head type set in Friz Quadrata

Printed and Bound in the United States of America
by McNaughton and Gunn, Inc. of Ann Arbor, Michigan

Pomegranate Press, Ltd.
3236 Bennett Drive
Los Angeles, California 90068

By the same author

A GUIDE TO LAUREL AND HARDY MOVIE LOCATIONS (1982)

FOLLOWING THE COMEDY TRAIL (1984)

Updated and reprinted in a new edition: FOLLOWING THE COMEDY TRAIL: A GUIDE TO LAUREL AND HARDY MOVIE LOCATIONS: 1988

The Thomas Bros. Map references listed throughout this text refer to coordinates in the current edition of The Thomas Guide, Los Angeles County Street Atlas and Directory, which is on sale at most Los Angeles stationery and book stores, or can be ordered by mail from :

Thomas Bros. Maps and Books,
603 West Seventh Street
Los Angeles, CA, 90017,
Telephone (213) 627-4018.

ACKNOWLEDGEMENTS

Many, many thanks to:

The Academy of Motion Picture Arts and
Sciences
    Robert Cushman

The Burbank Historical Society
    Ellen Dibble

The Glendale Public Library
    Barbara Boyd

The Los Angeles City Bureau of Engineering
    Alma Carlisle

The Los Angeles City Department of Airports
    Del Lyles
    Sam Montoya

The Los Angeles City Motion Picture
Coordinating Office
    Dirk Beving

Photoking Lab. Hollywood
    Cathy and Eric King

Universal City Studios, Inc.
    Richard Sullivan

USC/Warner Film Archives
    Leith Adams

Variety Arts Center
    Dorothea Brown
    James Fedorchak
    Milt Larsen
    Richard Mentzer

Warner Bros.
    Rob Friedman
    Judith Singer

And:
    Bob Bonday
    Michael Hawks
    Donald Key
    Tinsley Yarbrough
    Marcy Robin

A very special thank you to airport historian John Underwood, and to Jim Walters, a Laurel and Hardy and Our Gang film buff who possesses the eye of an eagle.

This book is respectfully dedicated to my wife Georgia and to Katherine Marie.

Detective Leon Smith in front of Parker Center,
Los Angeles Police Department Headquarters,
which was also a location in the DRAGNET films

Detective Leon Smith, a 30-year veteran of the Los Angeles Police Department, guides us on a nostalgic journey to famous Hollywood movie and TV locations. His investigations reveal exact addresses of these historical sites and feature his present-day photographs along with production stills showing how the locations appeared in the original film.

Leon Smith is a life-long movie buff with a special interest in discovering and photographing Los Angeles film locations. He's a writer, photographer, and film and book critic.

In his third book on this fascinating subject, Leon Smith lists scores of historic motion picture locations from Hollywood's "Golden Age" as well as sites in more recent motion picture and television series productions.

Have you ever wondered where King Kong held Fay Wray captive in the 1933 classic, where the immortal actor James Dean gave his all in REBEL WITHOUT A CAUSE in 1955, or the location of the gaping tunnel containing giant ants that threatened the city of Los Angeles in the horror classic THEM! in 1954? They're all in this book!

The scope of Smith's in-depth research encompasses Los Angeles County from the San Fernando Valley south to Long Beach and from the Pacific Ocean marinas to the streets and alleys of East Los Angeles.

To confirm the authenticity of each site, Smith has personally visited all locations included in this book. And he provides the address of each location to benefit those fans who may also plan a visit.

AUTHOR'S NOTES

The title of this book refers only to the physical locations in and near the city of Los Angeles utilized by motion picture and television production companies to film segments of motion pictures and television series that have appeared worldwide for decades, and is in no way connected with any firm or individual doing any type of business under this title or a similar title.

All locations listed in this publication have been identified through review of films, videotapes, still photographs taken at the time of filming, printed matter relating to the motion picture and television series production and the in-person viewing of the filming of a motion picture and/or television series. If you visit these locations, please remember that most of the residences are occupied and, of course, are private; and that many of the commercial properties restrict entry without permission. So please use discretion and courtesy. Do not trespass on private property or disturb the privacy of any person.

Also keep in mind that many locations are close to other locations. So to avoid back-tracking, review the locations carefully before a visit. For example, the THEM! tunnel is just down the street from the PENNIES FROM HEAVEN location; the Los Angeles City Hall (SUPERMAN) is only a few yards from the Parker Center Police Building (DRAGNET); Media Park (LAZY DAYS) is across the street from the car dealership where HIGHWAY TO HEAVEN was filmed which, in turn, is across the street from the historic Grant Tinker/Gannett Studios, which is just around the corner from the HONKEY DONKEY alley.

Take your time and plan your visit well. To help you, I've included references to Thomas Bros. Maps, which I highly recommend to anyone who undertakes this adventure.

Leon Smith

PREFACE

The Eiffel Tower in Paris, France is commonly credited with being the most photographed object in the world, closely followed by Cinderella's Castle at Disney World in Florida. And, without question, the most photographed city in the world is Los Angeles, California.

From the dawn of the motion picture industry in the Hollywood section of that city, production companies sought and found "authentic" locations - or those that seemed so to patrons of the perpetually filled movie theaters across the nation and in many foreign countries. This tradition continued with television production companies.

It was through those efforts that many Los Angeles boulevards, streets, neighborhoods, buildings and skyscrapers are recognizable to millions of movie fans. It was inevitable that such an extensive exposure generated a continual flow of tourists to stand where the "greats" exposed their talents to the camera.

Many motion picture/television locations can be found quite easily. Others are extremely difficult to find. Some have changed little over the past seven decades while more recent locations are hard to recognize, even with a description and directions.

Amazingly, Errol Flynn's Sherwood Forest is intact, looking much as it did in 1938 when he played Robin Hood. And the entrance to the

Looking west from Hill Street toward the 3rd Street tunnel.
Angel's Flight was located on the left side of the tunnel,
the stairs on the right.

The stairway seen in both NIGHT HAS A THOUSAND EYES (1948)
and THE GLENN MILLER STORY (1954).

Clay Alley as seen in THE GLENN MILLER STORY (1954).

Looking south from 2nd Street, just above Hill Street, at the site of the entrance to Clay Alley.

underground kingdom of "Murania" from Gene Autry's serial THE PHANTOM EMPIRE (1935) is unchanged - minus, of course, Mascot Studio's false rock door. This film site is only a few yards from the lair where King Kong held Fay Wray captive in 1933.

The famous cobblestone streets where Sherlock Holmes and Dr. Watson solved many crimes twist through a make-believe London, not far from the turf of Frankenstein, Dracula, the Mummy and the Wolf Man. And the terror continues just around the corner at the Bates Motel and the nearby Bates Mansion that Norman Bates shared with his "mother" in the PSYCHO series.

Boris Karloff's DEVIL'S ISLAND (1939) looms close to television's FANTASY ISLAND, which is across a placid lagoon from Tarzan's jungle where Johnny Weissmuller reigned as king during the 1930s and 1940s.

Many more sites are scattered across Los Angeles such as the railroad tracks where Oliver Hardy chased Stan Laurel in the closing scene of the comedy classic BERTH MARKS (1929), the rolling terrain where mounted apes chased and caught humans in the PLANET OF THE APES (1968), the town square and the long stairway Kevin McCarthy and Dana Wynter ran from and to in the 1956 horror classic INVASION OF THE BODY SNATCHERS, the park where James Dean loitered in REBEL WITHOUT A CAUSE (1955), the M*A*S*H encampment from the movie and the television series, an alien planet the crew of the starship Enterprise trod upon in a STAR TREK episode, and the twisting roads, trails and the landscapes seen perpetually in over 2,000 westerns.

These world-famous sites are yours to enjoy. The following pages list and depict locations of 198 motion pictures and 64 television series filmed at 73 "Hollywood" locations, plus seven historic movie studios and three famous movie ranches.

Many locations of historic significance, including motion picture/television series locations in the Los Angeles area, have been replaced by skyscrapers or parking lots. Some are defined by brass plaques firmly affixed to the side of a building or wall. But far too many are - and will remain - unmarked, and are lost forever. The most blatant examples are the site of the very popular tourist attraction Angel's Flight (the world's shortest railway that served the citizens of Los Angeles from 1901 to 1969), and the barely noticeable Clay Alley that ran beneath it, connecting 2nd and 4th Street in downtown Los Angeles.

Drawing on my memories as a life-long movie buff, I recall Edward G. Robinson hurrying down the long stairs parallelling Angel's Flight from Clay Alley to Hill Street in NIGHT HAS A THOUSAND EYES (1948). I also recall James Stewart walking up the same stairs to the pawn shop at Clay Alley in the opening scene of THE GLENN MILLER STORY (1954), and the many trips Stewart and Henry (Harry) Morgan took down Clay Alley toward 2nd Street in Morgan's automobile in the same motion picture. The building where I once worked was seen briefly in several scenes as Stewart and Morgan drove by.

Clay Alley no longer exists. It has been replaced by a massive apartment building complex that also claimed Angel's Flight. No landmark can be found at this location to remind one of a part of Los Angeles/motion picture history. And the most avid fan, without guidance, could not recognize this location of two motion picture classics. The photographs on page 11 and 12 prove my point.

Thomas Bros. Map reference: Page 44, D3.

CONTENTS

MOTION PICTURE INDEX

TELEVISION SERIES INDEX

MISCELLANEOUS INDEX

HISTORIC HOLLYWOOD MOTION PICTURE STUDIOS

HISTORIC MOVIE RANCHES

LOS ANGELES HISTORY

MOTION PICTURE AND TELEVISION SERIES LOCATIONS

The Hollywood Bowl as seen in A STAR IS BORN.
Janet Gaynor and Fredric March.

A STAR IS BORN

A Hollywood landmark.

The world-famous Hollywood Bowl has been a "natural" for location filming since the early 1930s. The best remembered scene filmed here for this classic motion picture was when an inebriated Fredric March continually disturbed the audience and caught the atten-tion of Janet Gaynor and her escort, Andy Devine.

The Bowl also was the setting for HOLLYWOOD HOTEL (1937), THREE SMART GIRLS (1937) and XANADU (1980) as well as for seg-ments of television's MANNIX and THE BEVERLY HILLBILLIES.

The Hollywood Bowl, 2301 N. High-land Avenue, is north of Franklin Avenue and west of the Hollywood Freeway (101) in Hollywood.

Thomas Bros. Map reference: Page 34 at B 2.

Errol Flynn dueling in the lake.
From THE ADVENTURES OF ROBIN HOOD.

THE ADVENTURES OF ROBIN HOOD

Robin Hood's lake and the cement bluff where many a hero and
bad guy fell into the water.

Surprisingly, the Sherwood Forest of this Errol Flynn classic still stands some forty miles from downtown Los Angeles on the grounds of the old Corrigan Ranch in the small community of Simi Valley.

Within the forest is the lake Flynn fell into, the result of an altercation with Alan Hale (Little John) and a botched piggyback ride with Eugene

Robin Hood's Sherwood Forest.

Pallette (Friar Tuck). The lake - a man-made cement basin - is now dry, allowing a view of the once waterproof camera housing room at its west end which was used to film underwater scenes. A cement bluff on the lake's north shore once served as a location for fight scenes in other movies; the bad guys (and occasionally the good guys) fell from it into the water as did buckboards and horses at the conclusion of exciting chase scenes.

Literally hundreds of Hollywood features were filmed at this location, mostly westerns by Monogram, Republic and PRC Studios which include Roy Rogers' COWBOY AND THE SENORITA (1944), ALONG THE NAVAJO TRAIL (1945), SUSANNA PASS (1946), DOWN DAKOTA WAY (1949) and TWILIGHT IN THE SIERRAS (1950); Gene Autry's HILLS OF UTAH (1951); Ken Maynard's HARMONY TRAIL (1944).

The Corrigan Ranch (now known as Hopeville) is an exciting part of Hollywood history that one hopes

Errol Flynn in Sherwood Forest.

Room at end of lake used to house camera equipment for underwater shots.

will be preserved for decades to come.

The ranch is on Kuehner Drive at Smith Road, south of the Simi Valley Freeway (118) in Simi Valley. The Sherwood Forest is at the east end of the ranch. It can be reached by driving east on Smith Road to its end, then east on a dirt road to the ranch gate. Once past the gate, continue east to the forest and the cement lakebed.

Thomas Bros. Map reference: Ventura County Book, Page 67.

The end of the road for many exciting chase scenes.

THE ANNIHILATOR

The 2nd Street tunnel facing Figueroa Street.

Many motion picture production companies regularly use the streets of Los Angeles to create a sense of reality that could be a part of the past, present, or far into the future. Thus many landmarks are utilized that could suggest any year or even any decade. The downtown tunnels that guide traffic from one side of the Bunker Hill area to the other are a good example.

The 2nd Street Tunnel was used as a location for a dramatic chase scene in this television movie. The tunnel was also seen in ONE DARK NIGHT (1983), THE TERMINATOR (1984), HEARTBREAKERS (1985), POLICE STORY: THE FREEWAY KILLINGS (1987) and THE NIGHT THAT PANICKED AMERICA, the 1975 television production based on Orson Welles' famous radio broadcast THE WAR OF THE WORLDS, which shocked America on the evening of October 30, 1938. The tunnel was also the setting for scenes for television's HEART OF THE CITY (1986), DOWNTOWN (1986) and JAKE AND THE FATMAN (1987).

The 2nd Street Tunnel is beneath the Bunker Hill section of downtown Los Angeles, between Hill Street and Figueroa Street.

Thomas Bros. Map reference: Page 44 at D 2 and 3.

BEING THERE

The Craven Estate main entrance seen from the parking area.

The Craven Estate House.

The city of Pasadena, California is a community that seems lost in time. Beautiful homes, mansions, and buildings of decades ago are as common as condos and townhouses in other cities across the nation. Therefore, motion picture production companies will obviously utilize such settings to suggest a bygone era. Recently, many television series production companies have followed, finding the community to be exactly right for their films.

The beautiful Craven Estate is a favorite. It is evident in this film wherein the late Peter Sellers gave one of his most memorable performances as a man with childhood innocence whose sole knowledge of life is based on what he sees on television, who becomes a person of prominence, prompted by the desperate need of people to believe in someone.

This was also the location for the film

MEMORY OF EVA RIKER in 1979, and scenes from the television series BIONIC WOMAN and MURDER, SHE WROTE.

The estate's address is 430 Madeline Avenue, west of Orange Grove Boulevard in Pasadena.

Thomas Bros. Map reference: Page 26 at F6.

BEVERLY HILLS COP

The City Hall as seen in BEVERLY HILLS COP and
BEVERLY HILLS COP II.

Nearly every COLBY fan knows that the Colby Mansion is Barron Hilton's West Los Angeles home. But few know that the stately building in the opening logo is the Beverly Hills City Hall. Every Eddie Murphy fan, I'm sure, is vividly aware that the building was the one their hero walked in and out of many times in BEVERLY HILLS COP (1984) and BEVERLY HILLS COP II (1987).

Television viewers may be interested to learn that the DALLAS mansion is near Piano, Texas, just outside Dallas. A duplicate mansion, complete with swimming pool, is located *inside* Sound Stage # 23 on the old M-G-M lot, now Lorimar-Telepictures.

The Beverly Hills City Hall, 450 N. Crescent Drive, is at the intersection of Santa Monica Boulevard in Beverly Hills.

Thomas Bros. Map reference: Page 33 at C 6.

BLOCK-HEADS

The escape route as seen in the final segment of the film.

This film was originally planned as the last in the career of Laurel and Hardy. It was not; an additional twelve features followed, but this entry is the last "vintage" comedy the team made.

Location filming began in the vast expanse of the Veterans' Administration complex in West Los Angeles and ended near downtown Los Angeles, near Westlake (MacArthur) Park.

The closing scene shows Stan and Ollie running between two buildings, closely followed by Billy Gilbert, who was firing at them with a shotgun. Hal Roach Studios also used this location in 1928 to film a similar scene for the Laurel and Hardy short WE FAW DOWN.

The buildings are the St. Arthur Apartments, 2014 W. 8th Street, and The Westmont, 807 S. Westlake Avenue, east of Alvarado Street, south of Wilshire Boulevard near downtown Los Angeles.

The film location was in the open area behind (west of) The Westmont and east of the St. Arthur Apartments, looking south from 8th Street.

Thomas Bros. Map reference: Page 44 at B 2.

The St. Arthur and the Westmont apartment buildings.

The famous farewell scene in front of the hangar.

CASABLANCA

The hangar as it is today.

Humphrey Bogart's famous farewell to Ingrid Bergman in the closing scene of this classic was filmed at the Los Angeles Metropolitan Airport, now the Van Nuys Airport. The hangar still stands but is no longer a part of the airport complex. Sold many years ago, it is now occupied by a shipping company. Its address, 16217 Lindbergh Street, is deceptive. The rear of the building - the hangar's entrance in 1942 - was the film site. It faces Waterman Drive, which in 1942 marked the beginning of the original runway and is now a narrow street bordering the realigned airport property.

Immediately west of the "farewell" building is another famous airplane hangar. It was also used briefly in CASABLANCA but played a much more important part in Laurel and Hardy's FLYING DEUCES (1939). The art-deco control tower, called the "radio tower" in the opening and closing scenes of CASABLANCA,

The airport arrival scene before it became Waterman Drive.

also appears in FLYING DEUCES (see that section for further information and photo). It was later seen in Chapter Nine of the Dead End Kids serial, JUNIOR G-MEN (1940).

The Van Nuys Airport is west of Woodley Avenue, between Roscoe Boulevard and Vanowen Street. The address is 6590 Hayvenhurst Avenue, Van Nuys.

The "farewell" building is on the south side of Waterman Drive, west of Woodley Avenue.

Thomas Bros. Map Reference:
Page 14 at F5 (Airport entrance)
Page 15 at A2 (Hangar location)

The old runway as seen in the film, now Waterman Drive.

Cast and crew filming the arrival scene.
Note the hangars in the background.

CHARLIE'S ANGELS

Burton Chace Park with Marina Del Rey in the background.

Boats tied up at the docks at Marina Del Rey.

The fishing shack, park and picnic area of Burton Chace Park provide attractive nautical backdrops for many television productions, including this popular series as well as FANTASY ISLAND, CHIPS, SIMON & SIMON (1986) and SPIES (1987). The dock and park were also seen in the motion picture OBSESSIVE LOVE (1984) that starred Yvette Mimieux and Simon MacCorkindale. The park and fishing dock are at the west end of Mindanao Way in the Marina Del Rey section of Los Angeles.

Thomas Bros. Map reference: Page 49 at E 5.

A view of the shoreline of the reservoir as seen
in CHINATOWN (1974) and OUT OF BOUNDS (1986).

CHINATOWN

The Hollywood Reservoir, in the Hollywood Hills above the film capitol of the world was dedicated in 1925, part of a vast network of waterways that provide the city of Los Angeles with water. This single reservoir serves more than 400,000 residents daily.

In CHINATOWN, private eye Jack Nicholson, who specializes in divorce cases, gets set up in the multi-million dollar land grab scandal in which many corrupt city officials are involved in diverting water to the City of Los Angeles.

Scenes from the film OUT OF BOUNDS were filmed here in 1986. In the disaster epic EARTHQUAKE (1974), the reservoir threatened to inundate Los Angeles.

The reservoir is east of the Hollywood Freeway (101) and east of Barham Boulevard at the terminus of Lake Hollywood Drive in Hollywood. Another approach from the opposite side of the reservoir is north of the Hollywood Freeway (101) and Franklin Avenue and east of Cahuenga Boulevard, at the end of Weidlake Drive in Hollywood.

Thomas Bros. Map reference: Page 24 at C 6 (Lake Hollywood Drive), Page 34 at C 1 (Weidlake Drive).

The dam that threatened the city of Los Angeles in EARTHQUAKE (1974).

CONDOR

4th Street viaduct spanning the Los Angeles River.

This made-for-television movie attempted to show what Los Angeles would look like in the year 1999. One of many locations, the Los Angeles River provided the backdrop for the exciting chase near the end of the film. The distant bridge that the hero's futuristic vehicle kept ap-proaching and approaching and ap-proaching is the 4th Street Viaduct. Lengthy as this chase scene was, neither the good guy's nor the bad guy's speedy car passed the viaduct. This was also the location for a seg-ment of television's THE OLDEST ROOKIE (1987).

Both scenes were filmed at the Los Angeles River, east of Santa Fe Avenue, between the 4th Street Viaduct and the 6th Street Viaduct in Los Angeles.

Thomas Bros. Map reference: Page 44 at E 4.

COPACABANA

The W. C. Fields bar.

Probably the best preserved film location of Hollywood's hidden past is in the heart of downtown Los Angeles - the Variety Arts Center.

This magnificent five-story structure, dedicated in 1924, is the first building in Los Angeles to use reinforced concrete as the mainstay.

That's why it has withstood many major earthquakes and has not succumbed to the wrecker's ball.

Variety Arts Center entrance.

Stage area of the roof garden ballroom as seen
in COPACABANA (1985).

More than a film location or a museum piece, the Variety Arts Center is dedicated to on-going performances of the acting profession. The film history contained within its walls is astounding and is arranged in a manner that allows one to enjoy Hollywood's past on any level of the building.

A few of the attractions are the Earl Carrol Lounge, the W. C. Fields Bar, the Masquers Theater, the Variety Arts Theater, the Music Library, the Theatrical Library, the Roof Garden Ballroom (seen in this film) and the

Motion picture and television production companies regularly use the premises for interior location filming. In this film, actor/musician Barry Manilow presents a gaudy salute to the lavish musicals of the 1930s.

Segments of television's CAGNEY & LACEY, FALCON CREST and MURDER, SHE WROTE were also filmed here.

Stage prop in the Ed Wynn Comedy Cellar that was seen in a
dance routine performed by Eleanor Powell in ROSALIE (1937).

Stairway of the Ed Wynn Comedy Cellar as seen in a HIGHWAY TO HEAVEN television production.

Ed Wynn Bar & Lounge, which was seen in a "back-in-time" episode of television's HIGHWAY TO HEAVEN.

The Variety Arts Center, 940 S. Figueroa Street, is east of the Harbor Freeway (110) in downtown Los Angeles.

The Variety Arts Center is a private establishment. Some areas are open to the public, some are not. Check in with the receptionist in the main lobby.

Thomas Bros. Map reference: Page 44 at C 4.

DIVINE MADNESS

The Pasadena Civic Auditorium.

This magnificent auditorium is the centerpiece of a complex that includes a conference building and an exhibition hall. The auditorium's majestic facade was used in Bette Midler's second movie, which, in fact, was a filmed concert. Portions of the film "10" were shot here in 1979.

The Pasadena Civic Auditorium, 300 E. Green Street, is between Arroyo Parkway and Los Robles Avenue in Pasadena.

Thomas Bros. Map reference: Page 27 at A 4.

DOUBLE INDEMNITY

The Hollywood Hills location used as Barbara Stanwyck's
home in this film.

This classic motion picture is based on James Cain's steamy novel of lust and greed involving an insurance agent's (Fred MacMurray) complicity in the murder of the husband of a lonely and lovely woman (Barbara Stanwyck). Early in the film, MacMurray drives up a winding street and stops at a beautiful Spanish-style house—the location of Stanwyck's home in the film. This Hollywood Hills setting overlooking the film capitol of the world, was chosen by Raymond Chandler who co-write the screenplay with Billy Wilder.

The house has changed little over the years, except for a more modern garage door.

Located at 6301 Quebec Drive, the house is at the intersection of Quebec Drive and El Contento Drive, north of Franklin Avenue in Hollywood.

Thomas Bros. Map reference: Page 34 at C 2.

Fred MacMurray and Barbara Stanwyck in Billy Wilder's
DOUBLE INDEMNITY which received seven Academy Award nominations.

Parker Center L.A.P.D. Headquarters.

DRAGNET

Jack Webb as Sgt. Joe Friday and Harry Morgan
as his partner, Officer Bill Gannon in the weekly television series.

Writer/producer/director/actor Jack Webb made the Los Angeles Police Department world famous with his characterization of Sgt. Joe Friday on radio and television from the 1940s to 1970. He used authentic locations as often as possible to give the viewers a sense of reality.

Early DRAGNET television episodes were filmed, in part, at the Los Angeles City Hall. Friday's police car exited and entered at the southeast corner of the building on Main Street, north of 1st Street. My father-in-law, George Mogelberg, employed by the City of Los Angeles, was a guard at that location and was often seen on episodes of the television series. He also appeared in scenes of the 1954 DRAGNET motion picture, also filmed at the Main Street location.

Exterior filming for both television and movie production shifted to the Police Administration Building (now renamed Parker Center in memory of the late Chief of Police William H. Parker) shortly after its dedication on September 12, 1955 and continued there until the series was canceled in 1970.

For interior shots, Webb faithfully recreated many areas of Parker Center in his Mark VII Ltd. production company at Universal Studios.

Entrance to Parker Center seen in both DRAGNET (1969) and DRAGNET (1987), as well as the DRAGNET television series.

Entrance to the Parker Center parking lot as seen in DRAGNET (1969) and the DRAGNET television series.

The detail was astounding; it was a replica of Parker Center that included the oak furniture and police-oriented wall decorations.

The 1987 DRAGNET motion picture was filmed, in part, at Parker Center. The Los Angeles Street public entrance and the San Pedro Street police entrance/exit appear in many scenes.

Webb also used the Georgia Street Juvenile Division building for many exterior and interior scenes for the television series. Originally the Georgia Street Receiving Hospital during and after World

The San Pedro Street entrance to Parker Center as seen in the DRAGNET television series and in DRAGNET (1987).

Parker Center is located at 150 North Los Angeles Street in downtown Los Angeles.

Thomas Bros. Map reference: Parker Center: Page 44 at D 3.
Thomas Bros. Map reference: Georgia Street Juvenile Building: Page 44 at B 4.

War II, it was converted to a juvenile facility in the early 1950s.

Deemed unsafe in case of a major earthquake, the building, now vacant and awaiting demolition, projects a nostalgic memory of Los Angeles' past.

Still intact as of this printing, the building is located at 1335 Georgia Street, south of Pico Boulevard, east of the Harbor Freeway (110) and north of the Santa Monica Freeway (10) near downtown Los Angeles.

The 1st Street exit from Parker Center as seen in DRAGNET (1969) and the DRAGNET television series.

Jack Webb and Ben Alexander in a scene from
an early DRAGNET TV episode.

Tom Hanks and Dan Aykroyd team up for the
1987 DRAGNET film.

The Georgia Street Juvenile Division building entrance
as seen in the DRAGNET television series.

Chico and Groucho, two of the Marx Brothers in DUCK SOUP.

DUCK SOUP

The magnificent entrance to Arden Villa as seen in ST. IVES.

In this Marx Brothers picture, the nation of Freedonia hires Rufus T. Firefly (Groucho) as a dictator in an effort to handle the threats of the neighboring nation of Sylvania. With the help of his three brothers (Chico, Harpo and Zeppo), Groucho involves Freedonia in a war with Sylvania which results in typical Marx Brothers shenanigans.

Scenes from this hilarious comedy were filmed at the Arden Villa, a 20,000-square-foot mansion in the heart of residential Pasadena. It has continued to be a popular motion picture and television series setting. Scenes for the Charles Bronson suspense yarn ST. IVES were filmed here in 1976, and scenes for the television series DYNASTY were

filmed here recently.

The Arden Villa, a private residence, is located at 1145 Arden Road, south of California Boulevard and east of Lake Avenue in Pasadena.

Thomas Bros. Map reference: Page 27 at C 5.

Franklin & Eleanor's "White House" in Pasadena.

ELEANOR AND FRANKLIN: THE WHITE HOUSE YEARS

The adjoining gardens.

Now the home of the Pasadena Historical Society, this beautiful mansion was used as a movie location as far back as 1912 by film pioneer D. W. Griffith. The surrounding grounds and gardens are extremely elegant and can easily propel one back in years, especially to the time of Franklin and Eleanor Roosevelt.

Other films shot at this location are THE QUEEN'S NECKLACE (1912), WESTERN LIFE (1918), and BEING THERE (1979). The building is located at 470 W. Walnut Street, south of the Foothill Freeway (210) in Pasadena.

Thomas Bros. Map reference: Page 26 at F 3.

Fantasy Island and the Queen Anne Cottage.

FANTASY ISLAND

In my perpetual search for movie locations, I have pinpointed the Los Angeles State and County Arboretum as the one location used by more motion picture and television production companies than any other on the face of the earth.

Since 1937, the grounds of the arboretum have provided a setting for more than one hundred motion pictures (many mentioned later in this book), and scores of television productions.

The television series most identified with this location is, of course, FANTASY ISLAND. The Queen Anne cottage, seen in all opening segments and throughout most episodes, is located beside the lagoon in the "Historical Area" of the 127-acre complex.

Although FANTASY ISLAND was filmed here from 1977 to 1982, the Queen Anne cottage was the principal set for the 1977 season only. The production company constructed a replica on their back lot in 1978, finding it more convenient to film there than to go on location each week with cast, crew and equipment.

The seaplane - which brought guest stars to Fantasy Island in the opening sequence of each episode - was moved to the arboretum lagoon by truck and placed in the water by crane.

Among the many television series filmed at this location are THE LOVE BOAT (1978), KNOTS LANDING (1982), DALLAS (1981), HART TO HART (1982) and DYNASTY (1984). The Los Angeles State and County Arboretum, 301 N. Baldwin Avenue, is south of the Foothill Freeway (210) in Arcadia.

Thomas Bros. Map Reference: Page 28 at C 4.

World famous Queen Anne cottage.

THE FLYING DEUCES

The Boys running from the hangar in an effort to escape.

The military airfield in this motion picture was actually the Los Angeles Metropolitan Airport, now the Van Nuys Airport. The art-deco control tower, prominent in many scenes, was demolished in the 1960s. Part of the "old" runway exists immediately west of the control-tower site. Both of these film locations are on airport property.

One of the airplane hangars still stands in its original location. It is now a privately owned machine shop. The address is 16205 Lindbergh Street, no longer a part of the airport complex.

The famous Laurel and Hardy scenes were filmed at the rear of the building (the hangar's entrance in

A different view of the same scene, showing
the art deco control tower in the background.

1939) which faces Waterman Drive, a narrow
street that borders the realigned airport
property. The film site is on the south side of
Waterman Drive, west of Woodley Avenue in
the Van Nuys area of Los Angeles.

The "old" runway seen in the film, looking west
from the site of the art deco control tower.

Art deco control tower seen in the film in a
photograph taken in the late 1930s.

Scenes for the motion picture DRAGNET
(1987) were filmed at the Van Nuys Airport,
and the L.A.P.D. jet airplane seen in that film
is presently housed there.

The hangar, the runway and the control
tower were also seen in Chapter Nine of the
Dead End Kids serial, JUNIOR G-MEN
(1940), and in the opening and closing scenes
of CASABLANCA (1942). Another hangar, immediately east of the one featured in THE
FLYING DEUCES, was the location of the
famous farewell scene from CASABLANCA.

A small airplane rests on the site of the
art deco control tower.

The hangar seen in the film in a 1929 photograph.

The hangar today.

The Van Nuys Airport is located west of Woodley Avenue, between Roscoe Boulevard and Vanowen Street. The address is 6590 Hayvenhurst Avenue, Van Nuys.

Thomas Bros. Map reference: Page 14 at F 5 (Airport entrance), Page 15 at A 2 (Hangar location).

Amber's mansion.

FOREVER AMBER

The entrance to Amber's garden.

The Greystone Mansion is surrounded by 18 acres of incredibly beautiful landscaped grounds, and I doubt that a more appropriate English manor house could have been found in Hollywood for this film that takes place during the reign of Charles II.

Once a part of the vast Doheny Ranch, the mansion was once the home of the American Film Institute. More than forty motion pictures have been filmed here over the years - notably, THE DISORDERLY ORDERLY (1964), THE LOVED ONE (1965), STRIPES (1981), and KILLER IN THE MIRROR (1986). The site was also used for segments of TV's THE INCREDIBLE HULK and MURDER, SHE WROTE.

The grounds (not the mansion) are open daily from 10:00 AM to 5:00 PM. There is no charge to visit. It's

Amber's garden.

also a popular setting for weddings, for which a fee is charged.

The mansion is located at 905 Loma Vista Drive, north of Sunset Boulevard in Beverly Hills.

Thomas Bros. Map reference: Page 33 at C 4.

More of Amber's garden.

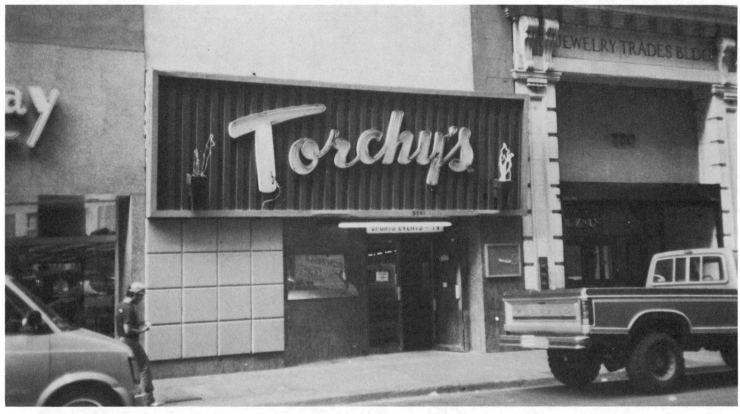

Torchy's.

Yes, Virginia, there is a "Torchy's Bar". It is in the heart of downtown Los Angeles - not Chicago, New York or a dozen odd other cities across the United States, which it has depicted in many feature films.

In this film, a San Francisco cop (Nick Nolte) gets wisecracking convict (Eddie Murphy) out of prison to help capture two killers. Torchy's is the red-neck joint they stumble into during their search. It was also the rather mild bar of the year 1999 in the 1986 film CONDOR, an indica-tion of its versatility as a film location.

The building is at 218 1/2 W. 5th Street in Los Angeles.

Thomas Bros. Map reference: Page 44 at D 3.

The Monster heading down cobblestone street
toward the arch seen in the "now" photo.

FRANKENSTEIN

Frankenstein's arch and town square seen in
FRANKENSTEIN (1931), THE WOLF MAN (1941) and MAGNIFICENT OBSESSION (1954).

Universal Studios, a major entertainment center and tourist attraction, has been producing motion pictures since 1913.

My favorite section on the lot is the "European Streets", constructed in 1931 for the original FRANK-ENSTEIN. Many of the same buildings and streets were used in the SHERLOCK HOLMES, DRACULA, MUMMY and WOLF MAN series films: THE BRIDE OF FRANKEN-STEIN (1935), THE WOLF MAN (1941), THE GHOST OF FRANKEN-STEIN (1942), SHERLOCK HOLMES AND THE SECRET WEAPON (1942), SHERLOCK HOLMES FACES DEATH (1943), THE SCARLET CLAW (1944), THE PEARL OF DEATH (1944), THE HOUSE OF FEAR (1945), HOUSE OF FRANK-ENSTEIN (1945), and TERROR BY NIGHT (1946).

Both photos are of buildings and streets seen in HOUSE OF DRACULA (1945) and FRANKENSTEIN MEETS THE WOLF MAN (1943).

This location was also the European village seen near the conclusion of MAGNIFICENT OBSESSION (1954), starring the late Rock Hudson, and as a medieval village in an award-winning 1987 episode of television's MOONLIGHTING.

This location is available only on the tram ride that takes visitors on a tour of the studio grounds.

The studio is located at 100 Universal City Plaza, north of the Hollywood Freeway (101) in Universal City.

Thomas Bros. Map reference: Page 23 at F 5.

Building seen in The Ghost of Frankenstein (1942).

The Monster on the roof of the building
in the "now" photo.

Buildings and arch seen in THE BRIDE OF
FRANKENSTEIN (1935) and Sherlock
Holmes' THE SCARLET CLAW (1944).

Building and arch seen in
HOUSE OF FRANKENSTEIN (1945).

Building and street seen in
THE GHOST OF FRANKENSTEIN (1942).

Shop seen in THE WOLF MAN (1941),
THE HOUSE OF FEAR (1945), and
TERROR BY NIGHT (1946).

Street and buildings seen in SHERLOCK HOLMES AND THE
SECRET WEAPON (1942) and SHERLOCK HOLMES FACES
DEATH (1943).

Street and building seen in THE PEARL
OF DEATH (1944).

GANGBUSTERS

The Los Angeles Police Academy entrance as seen in
THE ROOKIES (1972) and THE OLDEST ROOKIE (1987).

Portions of some early television programs were shot on location even though the studio was the primary location. It was fitting that the Los Angeles Police Academy athletic field was selected for the logo of GANGBUSTERS. A graduating class of uniformed police officers, tramping to cadence, soon became the program's familiar trademark.

Segments of SLEDGE HAMMER! (1986), THE OLDEST ROOKIE (1987), HILL STREET BLUES (1987), and the motion pictures THE NEW CENTURIONS (1972) and THE ROOKIES (1972) were filmed here.

One of the few remaining barracks buildings that housed athletes in the 1932 Olympic games is situated on the academy grounds. Now Classroom 7, it is located above the tiered parking area on the left (west) side of the entrance to the complex. The 1932 Olympic Village was originally located on the top of nearby Baldwin Hills.

The academy, 1880 N. Academy Drive in Elysian Park, is across the street from Dodger Stadium. There is an Academy Road exit on both the north and south lanes of the Pasadena Freeway (110) just north of downtown Los Angeles. Academy Road leads to Academy Drive.

Thomas Bros. Map reference: Page 35 at D 5.

The Los Angeles Police athletic field.

Entrance to classrooms at the Police Academy as seen in THE ROOKIES (1972).

A survivor of the 1932 Olympic games.

HART TO HART

As seen from the Macy Street Viaduct.

You've seen cars crushed by a massive press with the hero/heroine escaping in the nick of time or a massive forklift gouging out the windshield of the villain's onrushing Cadillac. Chances are, the scene was filmed at this spacious auto salvage yard near the Macy Street Viaduct east of downtown Los Angeles.

And hardly a month passes without motion-picture or television-series production companies descending on this popular location to capture yet another exciting demolition scene.

Scenes from this television series and many motion pictures include HUNTER (1986) and SIMON &

SIMON (1987).

The salvage yard is north of the Macy Street Viaduct, between Mission Boulevard and the Los Angeles River in East Los Angeles.

Thomas Bros. Map reference: Page 44 at F 2.

HI'-NEIGHBOR!

Fargo Hill - a 32% grade.

St. Teresa's Church.

In this Our Gang film, Wally (Wally Albright) wants to impress his girl (Jacqueline Taylor) and builds a "fire engine" from scratch to compete with a rich kid (Jerry Tucker) who has a custom-built fire engine.

As a race is about to begin, Jerry asks the Gang, "What's the matter, you afraid of a little hill?" Matthew "Stymie" Beard looks down the steep hill on which the engines are poised and replies: "What hill?"

The hill seen in a very brief shot is Fargo Hill, the fifth steepest street in Los Angeles; it has a 32% grade. The busy intersection at the base of the hill is at Glendale Boulevard and Fargo Street. The large building seen across Glendale Boulevard is St. Teresa's Church, 2210 Fargo Street.

Fargo Hill (Fargo Street) is between Allesandro Street and Alvarado Street, east of the Glendale Freeway (2) and south of the Golden State Freeway (5) in Los Angeles.

Thomas Bros. Map reference: Page 35 at C 4.

HIGHWAY TO HEAVEN

"Honest Eddie's" used car lot seen in the film.

If a movement is started to declare any American city a Hollywood" landmark, Culver City, California would win hands down.

Virtually surrounded by the City of Los Angeles, tiny 4.9 square-mile Culver City is packed with residential and business districts that have been used as motion picture/television locations for decades. Probably the most recognizable section of the city is the downtown area; several motion picture studios were located nearby and two still remain.

Motion picture locations in Culver City are listed throughout this book. Among the prominent television series filmed here was HIGHWAY TO HEAVEN, which aired in 1984 at Christmastime. The story, borrowed from Dickens' "A Christmas Carol", centers on "Honest Eddie" (Geoffrey Lewis), owner of a used-car lot, whose treatment of customers and employees puts "Scrooge" to shame.

This site is near the location of the film LAZY DAYS and across the street from the Grant Tinker/Gannett Studios, both of which are mentioned in this book.

The used car lot seen in the film is a used car/leasing area in downtown Culver City: 9099 W. Washington Blvd., at the southeast corner of Ince Boulevard and Culver Boulevard.

Thomas Bros. Map reference: Page 42 at C 6.

HONKEY DONKEY

The intersection of Bagley Avenue and
Venice Boulevard as seen in the film.

The HONKEY DONKEY alley between Bagley
Avenue and Cardiff Avenue.

In this Our Gang comedy, Wally's mother instructs her chauffeur (Don Barclay) to "take very good care of Wallace (Wally Albright) all the way home." But Wally has other ideas. He tells the driver to turn the limousine around and "drive through some alleys - some dirty ones."

The dirty alley the chauffeur finds is north of Venice Boulevard, between Bagley Avenue and Cardiff Avenue in Los Angeles. (The play area where Wally left the limo and encountered Our Gang was at the studio.)

Thomas Bros. Map reference: Page 42 at C 6.

HUNTER

Culver City City Hall.

P robably the most photo-graphed building in Culver City is its city hall. It is regularly seen in this television series as a police station. In 1932 it was a hospital in Laurel and Hardy's COUNTY HOSPITAL, and became a courthouse in their 1934 film GOING BYE-BYE! The building's address is 9770 Culver Boulevard, at the intersection of Duquesne Avenue in Culver City.

Thomas Bros. Map reference: Page 42 at C 6.

Alison Skipworth and W. C. Fields in the demolished car.

IF I HAD A MILLION

Site of the new car dealership and the
W. C. Fields' "crash scene"

The W. C. Fields segment of this classic film shows Fields having no luck at all driving the streets of Los Angeles. Throughout, he is either the victim of a traffic accident or the cause of one.

In the final scene, Fields and his wife (Alison Skipworth) exit the car dealership driving a new car. Fields looks both ways, then enters the street only to have his automobile

The address is 750 S. La Brea Avenue, at the intersection of La Brea and 8th Street, south of Wilshire Boulevard in Los Angeles.

Thomas Bros. Map reference: Page 43 at B 2.

Buildings on the south side of 8th Street, east of La Brea Avenue, Los Angeles as seen in the film.

demolished by a vehicle with the right of way.

The location was 8th Street, just east of La Brea. Buildings across 8th Street, seen in the film, remain unchanged since 1932. The car showroom was demolished and a new building is being constructed on that site.

Garage across 8th Street from the W. C. Fields' "crash site" as seen in the film.

Daisy's home on the Santa Monica pier.

Natalie Wood and Robert Redford star in this 30s film about the struggles of a star-struck girl determined to make it big in Hollywood. The charming Santa Monica Municipal Pier has been a favorite location of motion picture and television series production companies for decades because, with an appropriate camera angle and a prop or two, it can easily be transformed into a 1930s setting. Other films to take advantage of this location are THE GLENN MILLER STORY (1954) and THE STING (1973).

It's also doubled for other time periods, such as mid-fifties Los Angeles for the television movie PRIVATE EYE (1987), or the present day, as in THE BIG TRADE (1983). It was effectively used in television's CHARLIE'S ANGELS, MARCUS WELBY, M.D., CHIPS, SIMON & SIMON (1986) and HUNTER (1987).

INSIDE DAISY CLOVER and television's THREE'S COMPANY filmed at this location.

The electric car ride next to "Sinbad's" as seen in THREE'S COMPANY.

The pier was also seen in the motion picture STRANGE BARGAIN (1949), parts of which were incorporated into a 1987 episode of television's MURDER, SHE WROTE, featuring Martha Scott and Jeffery Lynn, who starred in the film.

The pier is probably best remembered from the opening and closing scenes of the 1980/1981 season of television's THREE'S COMPANY, which were filmed there in front of the famous Sinbad's and at the nearby electric bumper car ride.

The pier, at the end of Colorado Avenue, is west of Ocean Avenue in Santa Monica.

Thomas Bros. Map reference: Page 49 at A 6.

Kevin McCarthy and Dana Wynter on Sierra Madre Boulevard.

INVASION OF THE BODY SNATCHERS

Sierra Madre town square.

The city of Sierra Madre's town square (actually a triangle) served as the meeting place where residents (turned aliens) handled the famous pods. The hero (Kevin McCarthy) observed this ritual from the second story of a nearby medical building. Attempting to escape the human/aliens, McCarthy and his friend (Dana Wynter) pretend to be aliens. Leaving the building, Wynter tips their hand by displaying emotion (not the demeanor of an alien) when a dog wanders into the street and is nearly hit by a passing truck. McCarthy and Wynter run around the corner, down a street, up a flight of stairs, over hills, into a canyon, and finally find momentary safety in a cave.

The town square is virtually unchanged today, looking much as it did in the film. The medical building, however, was razed and replaced with a complex named Renaissance Plaza. The address is 38 W. Sierra Madre Boulevard.

When McCarthy and Wynter ran around the Sierra Madre corner - by the magic of the film cutter's art - they entered Belden Drive in the Hollywood Hills. Belden Drive led them to Westshire Drive, the street that led them to the flight of stairs. The stairs, 149 steps, begin between 2744 and 2748 Westshire Drive. They terminate between 2823 and 2831 Hollyridge Drive at Pelham Place. The hills McCarthy and Wynter traversed are the beginning of Bronson Canyon and yes, the canyon they entered was also Bronson Canyon.

The Sierra Madre town square is at the intersection of Sierra Madre Boulevard

Spanish style building across Sierra Madre Boulevard from "Renaissance Plaza" as seen in the film.

Building across Baldwin Avenue from the town square as seen in the film.

The beginning of the stairway, between 2744 and
2748 Westshire Drive as seen in the film.

Westshire Drive, east of the
building seen in the film.

Top of the stairway, between 2823 and 2831
Hollyridge Drive as seen in the film.

and Baldwin Avenue in Sierra Madre.
The Hollywood Hills location begins at
the intersection of Belden Drive and
Beachwood Drive, north of Franklin
Avenue and the Hollywood Freeway
(101) in Hollywood.

Thomas Bros. Map reference: Page 28 at C 2 (Sierra
Madre),
Page 34 at D 1 (Hollywood Hills).

The Body Snatchers chasing McCarthy and Wynter up Westshire
Drive in the 1956 film.

A view of the building and Westshire Drive as
seen in the film from the stairway.

Jimmy Stewart and Donna Reed dancing
in the gym above the swimming pool.

IT'S A WONDERFUL LIFE

The Beverly Hills High School gymnasium.

In this popular Frank Capra classic, the film's plot centers on the trials and tribulations of a young couple (James Stewart and Donna Reed) in the small town of Bedford Falls. Stewart and Reed, who attended Bedford Falls High School, later fall in love and are married. In a very humorous courtship scene, the two are dancing at a reunion at the high school gymnasium and innocently become victims of a prankster (Carl "Alfalfa" Switzer of Our Gang fame) who pushes a button which causes the dance floor — the basketball court above a swimming pool — to slowly open. As a result Stewart, Reed, and just about everyone else present either falls or jumps into the pool.

Beverly Hills High School opened in 1928, provided its gymnasium, completed in 1938, for the setting of the Bedford Falls High School reunion dance.

Beverly Hills High School is located at 241 S. Moreno Drive, north of Olympic Boulevard near the western boundary of Beverly Hills. The gym-

Beverly Hills High School.

nasium, however, is not part of the school building. It is located south of the complex, next to the school's athletic field at the intersection of Lasky Drive and Moreno Drive.

Thomas Bros. Map reference: Page 42 at B 2.

Beverly Hills High School.

The Bedford Falls Gymnasium dance floor/swimming pool as seen in the film.

Another view of the dance floor/swimming pool.

KING KONG

Bronson Canyon.

The entrance to the underground kingdom of Murania.

Bronson Canyon runs a close second to the Los Angeles State and County Arboretum as the location most photographed by motion picture and television production companies. The canyon (once a rock quarry that supplied early Los Angeles with stone for an ever-expanding streetcar network) is situated in vast Griffith Park.

Probably the most famous movie scene filmed here was in this classic. Another film of note that used the high Bronson Canyon walls was UNION PACIFIC (1939). In 1980, a segment of ALIEN'S RETURN was filmed here.

During the 1930s, Mascot Pictures used the canyon regularly for segments of their popular serials such as THE LIGHTNING WARRIOR (1931), MYSTERY MOUNTAIN (1934) and SHADOW OF THE EAGLE (1932).

One of Bronson's caves (caverns) became world famous as the entrance to the underground kingdom of "Murania" in the Mascot serial THE PHANTOM EMPIRE, the film that catapulted Gene Autry to stardom.

Television production companies also regularly used the canyon for segments of BATMAN, BONANZA,

King Kong on the Shrine Auditorium stage.

Details of the Shrine Auditorium.

The Shrine Auditorium.

GUNSMOKE and HAVE GUN-WILL TRAVEL, FANTASY ISLAND, OUTLAWS (1987) and STARMAN (1987).

Bronson Canyon is near the north end of Canyon Drive, north of Franklin Avenue, in Griffith Park. To reach the canyon one must walk approximately a quarter of a mile on a dirt road that runs east from Canyon Drive.

Thomas Bros. Map reference: Page 34 at D 1.

In 1933, another KING KONG location was the massive Shrine Auditorium, south of the downtown area, just across the street from the University of Southern California campus. This is the building in which the curious crowd assembled to see Kong in captivity.

The Shrine Auditorium was also used in SUNRISE AT CAMPOBELLO (1960) as the site of the 1932 Democratic National Convention that nominated Franklin D. Roosevelt (Ralph Bellamy) as presidential candidate.

I was present as a rookie police office during the filming in 1960, and I must admit that it was a special thrill; this was one of the first of many visits to motion picture and television locations that would follow over the years. On another memorable occasion, I was assigned to the security force that guarded Senator John F. Kennedy when he made a stirring speech at the Shrine Auditorium during his presidential campaign.

The Shrine Auditorium, site of the 1988 Academy Award presentations, is at the intersection of Jefferson Boulevard and Royal Street, west of the Harbor Freeway (110).

Thomas Brothers map refernce: Page 44 at A 6.

Details of the Shrine Auditorium.

LAZY DAYS

Location in the park where the majority of the scenes were filmed, with the Bagley Avenue and Venice Boulevard intersection in the distance.

Another view of the film location.

It is appropriate to the film's title that the setting would be a city park. In this Our Gang entry, Hal Roach Studios used nearby Media Park as a shady rest area for Allen "Farina" Hoskins and all of his Our Gang friends.

The park is down the street from the intersection of Venice Boulevard and Bagley Avenue, a location seen in the Laurel and Hardy films HATS OFF (1927) and BACON GRABBERS (1929), and in Our Gang's HONKEY DONKEY (1934).

Media Park is bounded by Canfield Avenue, Venice Boulevard and Washington Boulevard in Los Angeles.

Thomas Bros. Map referemce: Page 42 at C 6.

THE LOU GEHRIG STORY

The Pacific Asian Museum at 46 N. Los Robles, Pasadena.

The Pacific Asian Museum stands out like a jewel in a sea of sand. The museum was a prominent setting for this television film based on the heartbreaking true story of the baseball immortal afflicted with a rare and deadly disorder, now commonly known as Lou Gehrig's disease.

The Pacific Asian Museum, at 46 N. Los Robles Avenue, is north of Colorado Street in Pasadena.

Thomas Bros. Map reference: Page 27 at A 4.

MIDWAY

1151 Oxford Road, San Marino.

The world-famous Huntington Estate is in the heart of residential San Marino. The library, adjoining art gallery and botanical gardens are frequently used as locations for movie and television production companies. Scenes for this lavish reconstruction of the World War II air/sea battle that changed the course of the war were shot here. Scenes from AT LONG LAST LOVE (1975), THE BAD NEWS BEARS GO TO JAPAN (1978), and SCAVENGER HUNT (1979) were also filmed here.

The address is 1151 Oxford Road south of Orlando Road in San Marino. They are open to the public Tuesday through Sunday, 1:00 to 4:30 P.M.

Thomas Bros. Map reference: Page 27 at D 6.

Richard Masur, Richard Benjamin and Cloris Leachman
run through the gardens in SCAVENGER HUNT.

Marina del Rey from the wharf at Fisherman's Village.

MISSION: IMPOSSIBLE

More a television series location than a motion picture location, Fisherman's Village, with its Cape Cod-style buildings and adjoining docks provides an ideal setting for most waterfront scenes. It has been used mostly for TV series. Others filmed here were MOD SQUAD, THE F.B.I. and TRAPPER JOHN.

The village is located at 13723 Fiji Way in the Marina del Rey section of Los Angeles.

Thomas Bros. Map reference: Page 49 at E 6.

The lighthouse at Fisherman's Village.

THE MUMMY'S HAND

View of Universal's railroad station as seen in the films.

The ornate railway station at Universal Studios is still often used for "hello" (Gozinta*) or "goodbye" (Gozoutta*) scenes. Vintage movies that used this location include THE MUMMY'S HAND (1940), THE MUMMY'S TOMB (1942), TERROR BY NIGHT (1946) and SON OF FRANKENSTEIN (1939). In the latter, it became *Bahnhof Frankenstein*, the railroad station of the Frankenstein village. It was recently metamorphized into the railroad station of Wenton, Vermont in the opening and clos-

ing scenes of "Headless Horseman", a 1987 episode of MURDER, SHE WROTE.

The station is part of the "European Streets" section of the studio complex. Please refer to the FRANKENSTEIN section of this book for studio location.

* Show business terms often used by actors on the set.

Thomas Bros. Map reference: Page 23 at F 5.

Another view of the railroad station.

MURDER, SHE WROTE

6045 York Boulevard.

Police entrance to the station.

I f this building looks exactly like a police station, that's because it is (was).

The old Highland Park Police Station served that section of Los Angeles faithfully through two world wars and a lot of change. Replaced by the Northeast Area Police Station nearby, the building was bought by a motion picture company that leases it to other production companies seeking authentic exterior and interior shots of a police station.

The building is familiar to motion picture and television buffs not only as a Los Angeles police station, but as police stations in just about every major city in the nation. Scenes from the very popular MURDER, SHE WROTE and for the series Mac-GYVER (1986) were filmed here, as was Carol Burnett's FRESNO (1986).

The address is 6045 York Boulevard, near Figueroa Street, west of the Pasadena Freeway (110) in Los Angeles.

Thomas Bros. Map reference: Page 36 at C 1.

MY WICKED, WICKED WAYS

The Pasadena Railroad Station.

The Pasadena Railroad Station is familiar to movie viewers from the 1930s to the present as the locale for fledgeling movie stars arriving in "Hollywood" to seek fame. An example is the opening segment of this film on the early life of Errol Flynn.

The building is near the intersection of Del Mar Boulevard and Arroyo Parkway in Pasadena.

Thomas Bros. Map reference: Page 27 at A 4.

Amtrak's *Southwest Chief* at Pasadena.

NEVER GIVE A SUCKER AN EVEN BREAK

The Glendale-Hyperion viaduct.

Over the decades this comedy has been elevated to a cult status by film buffs due to the fact that the motion picture proved to be W. C. Fields' last starring role as well as one of his best performances before the camera.

Near the conclusion of the film, Fields drives his niece (Gloria Jean) to a department store. While awaiting her return he volunteers to rush a woman to a maternity hospital, thinking the woman is about to have a baby. The woman, heavy but not pregnant, was enroute to the hospital simply for a visit.

Most of the hectic drive to the hospital was filmed in East Los Angeles on and near the 7th Street Viaduct. Fields' car roared onto the viaduct at its east end and off at its west end, stopping at the intersection of 7th Street and Santa Fe Avenue to get directions from a traffic officer.

The street scenes filmed immediately thereafter were on Mission Road and on Santa Fe Avenue just north of the 7th Street Viaduct, between the viaduct and the 1st Street Viaduct. The west terminus of the 7th Street Viaduct is evident in the film, its distinctive decorative columns and railings prominent.

Today, however, the railings have been remodeled and the spaces between the railing posts filled with cement.

Farther on in this lengthy scene, Fields drives across a second bridge,

The 7th Street viaduct.

Intersection of 7th Street and Santa Fe Avenue.

his car coupled to the extended ladder of a fire engine that is racing to a fire. This film site is several miles west of the 7th Street Viaduct in the Atwater section of Los Angeles near the city of Glendale. This bridge is the Glendale-Hyperion Viaduct. Shortly after Fields crosses this bridge, the scene and the film ends

at the entrance to the maternity hospital, the result of a spectacular traffic accident.

The 7th Street Viaduct spans the Los Angeles River near the downtown district of Los Angeles. It is bounded by Myers Street on the east and Santa Fe Avenue on the west. The

Glendale-Hyperion Viaduct also spans the Los Angeles River as well as the Golden State Freeway (5). It is bounded by Greensward Road on the north and Ettrick Street on the south.

Thomas Bros. Map reference: Page 44 at E 5 and F 5 (7th Street Viaduct), Page 35 at B 2 (Glendale-Hyperion Viaduct).

The 4th Street Viaduct.

PENNIES FROM HEAVEN

West side of Santa Fe Avenue, under the 4th Street viaduct, Los Angeles.

East side of Santa Fe Avenue at the 4th Street Viaduct.

The majority of the outdoor scenes in this production were filmed at, near or under the 4th Street Viaduct at Santa Fe Avenue, east of downtown Los Angeles.

The plot of this film is the simple and tragic story of a restless salesman and the women in his life during the Depression days of the 1930s. The narrow viaduct underpass where stars Steve Martin and Vernel Bag-neris met the blind girl is on the east side of Santa Fe Avenue. The famous love scene in Martin's car between Martin and Bernadette Peters was filmed under the viaduct on the west side of Santa Fe Avenue, and was also the location at which the motorcycle policemen arrested Martin for the murder of the blind girl.

A few years later this location was a "San Francisco" street seen in a police pursuit in BADGE OF THE ASSASSIN (1985).

The film location is on Santa Fe Avenue, north of 6th Street and east of Alameda Street, beside the Los Angeles River.

Thomas Bros. Map reference: Page 44 at E 4.

PERFECT STRANGERS

The front of the "Ritz Discount Store" seen
often in each series segment.

In this popular television series, Balki (Bronson Pinchot) and Larry (Mark Linn-Baker) live and work in the same building in Chicago. The building's ground floor is the Ritz Discount Store, their place of employment, whose owner (Ernie Sabella) has a "going out of business sale" each month; Balki and Larry's apartment is in the hotel above.

This "Chicago" building is, in

Balki and Larry's apartment is on the third floor.

reality, the Santa Rita Hotel, a four-story brick building on the southern fringe of downtown Los Angeles, east of the Harbor Freeway (110) and north of the Santa Monica Freeway (10). The address is 1100 S. Main Street.

Thomas Bros. Map reference: Page 44 at C 4.

PIGSKIN PALOOKA

Front view of the Palms Station.

Side view of the Palms Station.

The Palms Railroad Station was the location where Our Gang met Carl "Alfalfa" Switzer when he returned from a military academy. Hal Roach also used the station as the "Pottsville" station in the closing scene of Laurel and Hardy's BERTH MARKS (1929).

The station is typical of the early railroad stations that dotted the Los Angeles landscape, and one of the few remaining wooden structures that date back to the steam railroads. It was fortunately rescued, relocated and restored before it became a victim of the wrecker's ball.

The Palms Station is now a permanent part of Heritage Square, the historical park dedicated to the recreation of Victorian Los Angeles from 1875 to 1915.

The Palms Station location signs were painted by railroad enthusiast Ward Kimball, formerly an animator for the Walt Disney Studios and a musician in the famed Firehouse Five Plus Two Dixieland Band.

Heritage Square is at 3800 N. Homer Street, east of the Pasadena Freeway (110) in Los Angeles.

Thomas Bros. Map reference: Page 36 at B 4.

The Palms Railroad Station at Heritage Square.

PLANET OF THE APES

It's a good forty-five minute drive from Hollywood, but it's worth every mile of the trip. Formerly the 20th Century-Fox Movie Ranch, the vast park was not only the wilderness in the original film in this series, a classic space adventure that goes sour, stranding confused astronauts on a planet where apes are the hunters and humans the hunted, but served as a beautiful location for HOW GREEN WAS MY VALLEY (1941), BUTCH CASSIDY AND THE SUNDANCE KID (1969), TORA! TORA! TORA! (1970) and the M*A*S*H (1970) movie and television series that followed.

The Malibu Creek State Park, is located Las Virgenes Road, south of Mulholland Highway in Calabasas.

Thomas Bros. Map reference: Page 107 at E 3.

Charlton Heston talking to actor Billy Curtis between takes.

Las Virgenes Road and Mulholland Highway, Calabasas.

The Malibu Creek State Park.

POLICE ACADEMY 2: THEIR FIRST ASSIGNMENT

3rd Street Tunnel facing Flower Street.

Another of Los Angeles' downtown tunnels, the Third Street Tunnel, served as a location for Steve Guttenberg and his partner to "take a break" from the trials and tribulations of the life of a police officer.

This film was the second in the series, depicting a herd of screwball cops who graduate from the Police Academy and immediately wreak

A scene from POLICE ACADEMY 2 filmed near the tunnel.

havoc on the citizens as well as the bad guys of the city.

The tunnel is beneath the Bunker Hill section of downtown Los Angeles, between Hill Street and Flower Street.

Thomas Brothers Map reference: Page 44 at D 3.

A very beautiful and magnificent Queen.

THE POSEIDON ADVENTURE

Entrance to the Queen Mary Hotel.

View along the promenade deck.

No Hollywood set could possibly provide the authenticity of the fabulous floating legend, the *Queen Mary*. It was only natural to utilize the ornate interior and exterior of this magnificent vessel to film scenes for this epic ocean-liner disaster motion picture of the liner S. S. Poseidon that capsizes on its final voyage from New York City to Athens, Greece.

Scenes were also filmed here for the features DEATH CRUISE (1974), THE EXECUTION OF PRIVATE SLOVIK (1974), UNDER THE RAINBOW (1981), THE LAST FRONTIER (1986), and SOMEONE TO WATCH OVER ME (1987), as well as the TV series NERO WOLFE, QUINCY, MURDER, SHE WROTE and TALES OF THE GOLD MONKEY.

The Queen Mary is permanently docked at Pier "J", south of the Long Beach Freeway (7), at the end of Harbor Scenic Drive.

Thomas Bros. Map reference: Page 80A at C 5.

A view along the boat deck.

One of the Queen's lifeboats with the container port
cranes in the background.

Norman approaching the Bates Mansion.

PSYCHO

The Bates Mansion.

The only access to the Bates Motel and the Bates Mansion is by tram at the Universal Studios. And when the tram stops beside the motel, one still feels that Norman Bates (Anthony Perkins) is glaring down from one of the main windows of the gloomy-looking mansion on the nearby hill.

The Bates Motel, now 27 years old, was recently opened for two winners of an unprecedented national contest to promote PSYCHO III. The "fortunate ones" spent the night in famous Cabin # 1. Yes, they survived and spent the following night at the nearby Sheraton Universal Hotel, the guests of Universal Pictures.

PSYCHO II (1983) and PSYCHO III (1986) were also filmed at this hallowed site, as was BATES MOTEL (1987), a television-movie sequel to the three PSYCHO thrillers.

Universal Studios, at 1000 Universal City Plaza, is north of the Hollywood Freeway (101) in Universal City.

Thomas Bros. Map reference: Page 23 at F 5.

The Bates Motel with the mansion in the background.

The Bates Motel in 1960. John Gavin and Vera Miles.

St. Brendan's Church.

PUPS IS PUPS

Entrance to church where "Wheezer" is reunited with his puppies in PUPS IS PUPS (1930), and "Spanky" and his family approached in BIRTHDAY BLUES (1932).

Our Gang member Bobby "Wheezer" Hutchins spends the first half of this Hal Roach comedy classic searching for his lost puppies. The puppies are trained to respond to bells, so, naturally, Wheezer rings every bell possible in an attempt to have a reunion.

The streets and sidewalks of the east side of downtown Los Angeles were the primary film sites. After nearly six decades, a stately brick wall paralleling a sidewalk seen in the film still stands, in part, on Center Street, between Ducommun Street and Commercial Street. Also intact

is a building used in the film across the street from an apartment house where "Wheezer" tosses a rock through a window that is visibly wired to a burglar alarm, hoping its sound will summon his puppies. The building is now an auto-repair shop at 749 E. Temple Street, on the

749 E. Temple Street, Los Angeles.

another Our Gang comedy. It is seen in the closing segment of BIRTHDAY BLUES (1932) as George "Spanky" McFarland, Dickie Moore, Hooper Atchley and Lillian Rich approach the entrance from the east side of Van Ness Avenue, immediately south of the church. In 1953, St. Brendan's was the church seen in the closing segment of the film WAR OF THE WORLDS.

Thomas Bros. Map reference: Page 44 at E 3 (brick wall and building), Page 43 at D 1 (church).

northwest corner of Temple Street and Center Street, south of the brick wall.

At the film's conclusion, Wheezer is reunited with the puppies on the steps of a church - thanks to the timely ringing of the church bells. The church is St. Brendan's. It is located many miles west of downtown Los Angeles at the intersection of Third Street and Van Ness Avenue in Los Angeles, west of the Hollywood Freeway. The film site (the entrance to the church) faces Van Ness Avenue, just south of Third Street.

Two years later, St. Brendan's was the setting for

Center Street and Commercial Street, Los Angeles.

Sidewalk, steps, houses and driveway on Van Ness
Avenue, south of the church as seen in BIRTHDAY BLUES (1932).

The immortal James Dean with the dome of the
observatory in the background.

REBEL WITHOUT A CAUSE

2800 E. Observatory Road (Griffith Park), Los Angeles.

Another Los Angeles landmark, the Griffith Observatory in Griffith Park, has served as a motion picture and television series location for more than fifty years. Of the many films shot there, this James Dean classic is by far the most popular with movie buffs. A lengthy Dean scene was filmed in front of the observatory building and featured the Astronomer's Monument. This 40-foot-high stone monument is dedicated to astronomers Sir William Herschel, Sir Isaac Newton, Johannes Kepler, Nicolaus Copernicus,

Galileo Galilei and Hipparchus. Cast-stone figures of each astronomer surround the base of the monument, which was a WPA project of the 1930s. But those who come to the location hoping to find the bench on which Dean sat will be disappointed: it was replaced many years ago.

Among other motion pictures that

Murania's dome and wall.

Stairway leading into Murania.

used the location are THE DARK CITY (1950) and THE TERMINATOR (1984). The observatory building was part of the undersea kingdom of Murania in the Mascot serial THE PHANTOM EMPIRE (1935). Scenes for television's BIONIC WOMAN, BATTLESTAR GALACTICA and, more recently, THE COLBYS (1987) were also filmed there.

Brass art deco and wall of Murania.

The observatory is in Griffith Park at 2800 E. Observatory Road, north of Los Feliz Boulevard in Los Angeles.

Thomas Bros. Map reference: Page 34 at E 1.

The astronomer's monument as seen in James Dean's REBEL WITHOUT A CAUSE (1955).

ROCKY

Motion picture production companies found the ideal setting for boxing films at the Olympic Auditorium near downtown Los Angeles. Dedicated on August 5, 1925, the building had an original seating capacity of 15,300, making it the largest auditorium ever built specifically for boxing in the western United States.

As expected, scheduled events attracted a steady flow of Los Angeles citizens - including many show-biz greats from Al Jolson to Sylvester Stallone, who would eventually star in this film and the successful sequels that followed. Many of Stallone's boxing scenes were shot here, as were scenes from REQUIEM FOR A HEAVYWEIGHT (1962).

The Olympic Auditorium, 1801 S. Grand Avenue, is south of the Santa Monica Freeway (10) and east of the Harbor Freeway (110).

Thomas Bros. Map reference: Page 44 at B 5.

The auditorium entrance on Grand Avenue.

A view of the auditorium from the intersection
of 18th Street and Grand Avenue.

Eddie Cantor in a chariot approaching the bridge
in ROMAN SCANDALS.

ROMAN SCANDALS

The Colorado Street Bridge as seen in the film.

United Artists used many locations throughout greater Los Angeles in this Eddie Cantor comedy classic. One was the Colorado Street Bridge, dedicated in 1913. This magnificent structure was, for decades, a vital link between the city of Pasadena and its neighbor, Los Angeles. It spans the beautiful Arroyo Seco, a spacious parkway that continues north to the world famous Rose Bowl.

The bridge gained international fame when audiences saw Eddie Cantor drive his chariot over its arches. Later in the 1930s it was known as " Suicide Bridge" - a dubious claim to fame. To date, nearly 100 deaths have resulted from leaps from its lengthy span.

Colorado Boulevard is a main traffic artery that bisects the city of Pasadena from east to west. The bridge is west of Orange Grove Boulevard and immediately south of the Ventura Freeway (134) in Pasadena.

Thomas Bros.Map reference: Page 26 at E 4.

The Colorado Street Bridge.

The Colorado Street Bridge.

THE ROSE BOWL STORY

1001 Rose Bowl Drive, Pasadena.

The Rose Bowl is located at 1001 Rose Bowl Drive, south of the Foothill Freeway (210) in Pasadena.

Thomas Bros. Map reference: Page 26 at E 2.

The Rose Bowl, a landmark in Pasadena, be-comes an attraction in the sports world each New Year's Day. It is also a favorite location for motion picture and television production companies. Segments of this motion picture were filmed here in 1952 - as were segments of EVEL KNIEVEL (1971), and televison's THE ROOKIES, S.W.A.T., CANNON and THE SIX MILLION DOLLAR MAN.

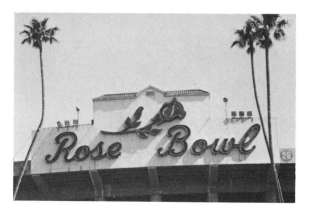

The Rose Bowl.

The playing field.

SHERLOCK HOLMES IN WASHINGTON

View of terminal as seen in the films.

In the opening scene of this film, a passenger aircraft is preparing to fly from London to Lisbon. A stately palm tree is evident near the London Terminal of Transatlantic Airways. Very odd indeed for London. But not for California!

The "London Terminal" was the Grand Central Airport in Glendale, also the location for the opening scenes of HOLLYWOOD HOTEL (1937). The complex long ago faded into local history; the property is now an industrial park. But the control tower still exists, virtually unchanged from the airport's heyday in the 1930s and 1940s.

The Glendale control tower and airport have - erroneously - been identified as the site of Laurel and Hardy's THE FLYING DUECES (1939). Although both control towers are similar, the one seen in THE FLYING DEUCES has one set of windows on each side; the control tower in the SHERLOCK HOLMES film has two sets. The FLYING DEUCES tower (now

Glendale's Grand Central Airport Terminal.

Dr. Watson and Holmes look over some evidence in
SHERLOCK HOLMES IN WASHINGTON.

Grand Central Airport Terminal.

demolished) was at the Van Nuys Airport, many miles west of the Glendale Airport. (Please refer to the FLYING DEUCES section of this book.)

The control tower of Glendale's Grand Central Airport is at 1310 Air Way, east of the Golden State Freeway (5) in Glendale.

Thomas Bros. Map reference: Page 24 at F 2.

SLEDGE HAMMER!

The police station where Sledge toiled to protect
the citizens of Los Angeles.

Detective Sledge Hammer (David Rasche) and his partner (Anne-Marie Martin) prowled the streets of Los Angeles in pursuit of the "baddies".

This tongue-in-cheek television police comedy was primarily filmed in the Los Angeles area. The building most familiar to viewers was Sledge's apartment: he seldom went there during the day, but nearly always slept in at night, cuddling his chrome-plated, pearl-handled .357 Magnum. Sledge's home throughout the series was 681 S. Burlington Avenue, north of 7th Street and west of the Harbor Freeway (110), near downtown Los Angeles.

The "police station" - an office building that has withstood Sledge's antics - is one block north and nine blocks east of his apartment building.

Address of the police station/office building is 1125 W. 6th Street, west of the Harbor Freeway (110), in downtown Los Angeles.

Thomas Bros. Map reference: Page 44 at B 2 (apartment building), Page 44 at C 2 (police station).

Sledge Hammer's apartment building.

Laurel and Hardy at the old Santa Fe station
in the opening scene of BERTH MARKS.

SOMETHING TO SING ABOUT

Site of Santa Fe Railroad Station.

300 Santa Fe Avenue, Los Angeles.

In this film James Cagney, traveling from New York to California to begin a film career, arrives at the old Santa Fe Railroad Station - *the* place to arrive in Los Angeles before the opening of Union Station in the late 1930s.

Hal Roach used the station for opening scenes of Laurel and Hardy's BERTH MARKS (1929) and Our Gang's CHOO-CHOO! (1932). Recently, the location was seen in the television series WISEGUY (1987).

This location is truly a part of Hollywood history: the train carrying the body of screen immortal Rudolf Valentino from New York arrived there in 1926. (Valentino was later interred at the Hollywood Memorial Park Cemetery at 6000 Santa Monica Boulevard in Los Angeles; Thomas Bros. Map Page 44 at D 4).

The Santa Fe Station was long ago replaced by the Santa Fe Transportation Company, a trucking firm that was, in turn, replaced by the Southern California Rapid Transit District. The railroad yards and the main rail lines still exist on the property.

The film site is at 300 Santa Fe Avenue, south of the 1st Street Viaduct in Los Angeles.

Thomas Bros. Map reference: Page 44 at E 3.

The STAR TREK crew

STAR TREK

Cliff on an alien planet.

The Vasquez Rocks in Vasquez Rocks Park, ideal for the landscape of a distant planet, are used for segments of the "Shore Leave" episode of this popular television series.

A different camera angle creates a scene from the old West in scores of films such as Rocky Lane's BANDITS OF DARK CANYON (1947), Roy Roger's THE FAR FRONTIER (1948), LEGEND OF THE LONG RANGER (1981) and THE THREE KINGS (1987).

Mountain on an alien planet and Big Foot's home.

Western Badlands (Above).

Stagecoach Trail (Below).

The park was also a backdrop in a segment of the television series HELL TOWN (starring Robert Blake), and for two segments of FANTASY ISLAND, once as a prehistoric-earth setting and once for a "Big Foot" locale.

Vasquez Rocks Park is north of the Antelope Valley Freeway (14), at the intersection of Schaefer Road and Agua Dulce Canyon Road in the city of Agua Dulce.

Thomas Bros. Map reference: Page 188 at C 2.

SUNSET BOULEVARD

The Alto-Nido apartment building at 1851 N. Ivar, Hollywood.

A Spanish Colonial apartment building with a tile roof and wrought-iron balconies was needed for the home of an unemployed Hollywood screenwriter (William Holden).

The setting, seen near the opening of the film, is the Alto-Nido apartment building at 1851 N. Ivar Avenue, west of Vine Street and north of Yucca Street in Hollywood.

Thomas Bros. Map reference: Page 34 at C 2.

SUPERMAN

The Los Angeles City Hall is as familiar to motion picture and television series fans as the famous Hollywood sign. The architecture catches the eye of Angelenos and tourists alike. The interior of the building dates from a time of elegance, and often doubles for interiors of the Senate Office Building in Washington, D.C., and courtrooms.

The exterior, minus its peaked top, was the *Daily Planet* newspaper building of TV's popular 1950s SUPERMAN series. Interior shots of the building are seen in MILDRED PIERCE (1945), THE SUNSHINE BOYS (1975), GOING BERSERK (1983), Goldie Hawn's PROTOCOL (1984), BADGE OF THE ASSASSIN (1985), LBJ: THE EARLY YEARS (1987) and STILLWATCH (1987). The famous west entrance used in DRAGNET (1987) is also a site of historical importance: Gen. George S. Patton reviewed World War II troops from the top of the west-entrance stairway.

Many scenes for television productions were filmed here, including CAGNEY & LACEY, HILL STREET BLUES, HIGH-

The Los Angeles City Hall, a.k.a. ``The Daily Planet''

Corridor inside City Hall.

The City Hall's west entrance where Gen. Patton stood to review World War II troops. It was also seen in the DRAGNET television series and in the motion picture DRAGNET (1987).

The Olympic Cove seen in LBJ: THE EARLY YEARS.

City Hall garage exit on Main Street, north of
1st Street as seen in the early (1950s) DRAGNET television series.

WAY TO HEAVEN, THE COLBYS (1986), MATLOCK (1986), TWILIGHT ZONE (1986), L.A. LAW (1986), MURDER, SHE WROTE (1987), and JAKE AND THE FATMAN (1987).

The City Hall is at 200 N. Spring Street in downtown Los Angeles.

Thomas Bros. Map reference: Page 44 at D 3.

TARZAN ESCAPES

Tarzan's lagoon at the Los Angeles State
and County Arboretum.

Tarzan and his family crossing the lagoon in
TARZAN AND THE HUNTRESS.

The entrance to Tarzan's jungle.

The enchantment of the Los Angeles State and County Arboretum continues. Across the lagoon from the FANTASY ISLAND cottage is the "Prehistoric and Jungle Garden" section of the vast complex. And a lush jungle it is, complete with dense foliage of every description and, of course, Tarzan's vines.

Four Tarzan movies and other vintage films were shot here. The four Tarzan movies were: TARZAN ESCAPES (1936), TARZAN AND THE AMAZONS (1944), TARZAN AND THE LEOPARD WOMAN (1945) and TARZAN AND THE HUNTRESS (1946). Other motion pictures include DEVIL'S ISLAND (1938), THE ROAD TO SINGAPORE (1939), THE

Tarzan's jungle.

MAN IN THE IRON MASK (1939), GENTLEMAN JIM (1942) and PASSAGE TO MARSEILLES (1944).

Strolling along jungle paths, the imagination runs wild. One slips back into a carefree past when the Lord of the Apes was in command and wild animals (no longer present at the time of my visit) dutifully followed his commands.

The Los Angeles State and County Arboretum, at 301 N. Baldwin Avenue, south of the Foothill Freeway (210), is in Arcadia.

Thomas Bros. Map reference: Page 28 at C 4.

Johnny Weissmuller and Herbert Mundin in the jungle.

More of Tarzan's jungle.

Joan Weldon, Edmund Gwenn, and Onslow Stevens at the
entrance to the tunnel.

THEM!

Los Angeles River (movie) entrance.

West entrance from Santa Fe Avenue.

In this film, giant ants from the Mojave Desert swarm into Los Angeles and its massive storm-drain system. A young James Arness teams with James Whitmore and Edmund Gwenn to destroy the invaders before they reproduce and devastate the city.

The THEM! Tunnel, which runs directly under the 6th Street Viaduct, is an access to the Los Angeles River from nearby Santa Fe Avenue.

The access has become popular with producers of television movies and series recently. It was used on TV for THE ANNIHILATOR (1986) and CONDOR (1986), and segments of MOONLIGHTING (1986) and THE OLDEST ROOKIE (1987).

The film location is under the 6th Street Viaduct, east of Santa Fe Avenue, at the Los Angeles River channel in Los Angeles.

Thomas Bros. Map reference: Page 44 at E 4.

THREE'S COMPANY

The zoo's entrance at 5333 Zoo Drive (Griffith Park).

Another view of the zoo's entrance.

The Los Angeles Zoo provides motion picture and TV production companies with an authentic location. The opening titles of this extremely popular series were filmed here as were segments of THE INCREDIBLE HULK, CHIPS, THE BEVERLY HILLBILLIES and the motion picture BODY AND SOUL.

The "Los Angeles Zoo" sign, familiar from the opening titles of THREE'S COMPANY, was a casualty of the zoo's remodeling.

The zoo is located at 5333 Zoo Drive in Griffith Park, south of the Ventura Freeway (134) and west of the Golden State Freeway (5) in Los Angeles.

Thomas Bros. Map reference: Page 25 at A 3.

UNDER THE RAINBOW

9501 Culver Boulevard, Culver City.

The stately old Culver City Hotel, in the heart of downtown Culver City, has been seen in many motion pictures over the decades: Laurel and Hardy's PUTTING PANTS ON PHILIP (1927), Our Gang's HONKEY DONKEY (1934), and television's SLEDGE HAMMER! (1986).

In UNDER THE RAINBOW, the hotel was the meeting place for a group of midgets who were in "Hollywood" to audition for THE WIZARD OF OZ.

The hotel's address is 9501 Culver Boulevard, Culver City.

Thomas Bros. Map reference: Page 42 at C 6.

William Holden in Union Station lobby during filming of
a scene from UNION STATION.

THE WAY WE WERE

Main hall seen in the film (opposite). Note the wall tiles.

In the late 1930s, the magnificent Union Station replaced the Santa Fe Railroad Station as main passenger terminal for the Los Angeles area. Its architecture is perhaps the best example of what has been called "typical Californian." It provides the ideal World War II atmosphere for THE WAY WE WERE, a love story set against America's changing political landscape of the late 1930s through the early 1950s.

Scenes were also filmed here for the motion pictures UNION STATION (1950), GABLE AND LOMBARD (1975), UNDER THE RAINBOW (1981), and IN THE MOOD (1987), as well as the television movie PRIVATE

Union Station.

Entrance to the train area as seen in the films.

EYE (1987) and the television series SHELL GAME (1987).

Union Station, 800 N. Alameda Street, is north of the Hollywood Freeway (101) in downtown Los Angeles.

Thomas Bros. Map reference: Page 44 at E 2.

Union Station courtyard as seen in the films.

The clock tower.

The train platform area.

THE WHITE CLIFFS OF DOVER

The Victorian Bradbury Building.

The five-story Bradbury Building (1893) is a tribute to Los Angeles' Victorian past. Its ceiling is capped by a 50-foot by 120-foot skylight. The interior combines brick, tile and metal. Open-cage elevators give a view of the magnificent lobby as they slowly ascend to iron-grilled balconies opening onto numerous offices throughout the building.

Scenes from this film, starring Irene Dunne as an American marrying Alan Marshall, an English aristocrat who was eventually killed in World War I, were filmed here in 1944. Other movies that used the location were: D.O.A. (1949), GOOD NEIGHBOR SAM (1964), CAPRICE (1967), BANYON (1971) THE CHEAP DETECTIVE (1978), and BLADERUNNER (1981). It was also the setting for the Boston Blackie detective movies, starring Chester Norris. Among them: MEET BOSTON BLACKIE (1941), AFTER MIDNIGHT WITH BOSTON BLACKIE (1943), and BOSTON BLACKIE'S RENDEZVOUS (1945).

The Bradbury Building, now an office complex, is on the southeast corner of 3rd Street and Broadway in downtown Los Angeles.

Thomas Bros. Map reference: Page 44 at D 3.

The Bradbury Building at 3rd Street and
Broadway, Los Angeles

An 1890s hallway.

HISTORIC MOTION PICTURE STUDIOS

CHAPLIN STUDIOS

1416 N. La Brea Avenue, Hollywood.

The site of countless Charlie Chaplin comedies, the Chaplin Studios, when built in 1919, were reputed to be the "first complete motion picture studio in Hollywood."

The most popular films produced here were THE GOLD RUSH (1925), CITY LIGHTS (1931), MODERN TIMES (1936), and THE GREAT DICTATOR (1940).

The studio complex is at 1416 N. La Brea Avenue, south of Hollywood Boulevard in Hollywood. It is presently the home of a recording studio.

Thomas Bros. Map reference: Page 335 at B 2.

DISNEY STUDIOS

2725 Hyperion Avenue, Los Angeles.

The original Walt Disney Studio was built in 1926. Many outstanding animated cartoons and features of the 20s, 30s and 40s were filmed there: SNOW WHITE AND THE SEVEN DWARFS (1937) is probably the most memorable.

The studio was at 2719 Hyperion Avenue. Today, no sign of the original complex exists. A supermarket now occupies the area. Its address is 2725 Hyperion Avenue, east of Los Feliz Boulevard in Los Angeles.

Thomas Bros. Map reference: Page 35 at B 2.

GRANT TINKER/GANNETT ENTERTAINMENT STUDIOS

9336 W. Washington Boulevard, Culver City.

Built in 1919, the beautiful administration building of the Thomas H. Ince Studios became an overnight Culver City landmark. Over the years, it became part of a studio complex owned by RKO, Pathe, Desilu, and other production companies. The original building appeared as the logo behind the opening credits of many Selznick International Pictures productions, the most famous of which was the 1939 epic GONE WITH THE WIND.

A local historical society claims that the Selznick back lot was torched for GWTW's famous burning-of-Atlanta sequences. However, M-G-M Studios, a short distance away, is also credited with this honor. The mayor of Culver City recently stated that "Atlanta was burned on this site", referring to M-G-M's back lot, now a residential section of Culver City, immediately west of the old M-G-M Studio (now Lorimar-Telepictures).

The studio was recently purchased by Gannett Co., Inc., a publishing conglomerate, and is now known as Grant Tinker/Gannett (GTG) Entertainment. The sign on the facade of the administration building now reads THE CULVER STUDIOS.

The studio complex is located at 9336 W. Washington Boulevard, at the intersection of Ince Boulevard in Culver City.

Thomas Bros. Map reference: Page 42 at C 6.

METRO-GOLDWYN-MAYER STUDIOS

End of Grant Avenue, west of Madison Avenue, Culver City.

This famous motion picture studio has two entrances known to moviegoers worldwide. The "classic" entrance is on Washington Boulevard, west of Madison Avenue. The so-called "deco" entrance is at the end of Grant Avenue, west of Madison Avenue. This entrance was seen in the 1981 movie MOMMIE DEAREST that starred Faye Dunaway.

The studio was recently sold and is now Lorimar-Telepictures. The address is 10202 W. Washington Boulevard, Culver City.

Thomas Bros. Map reference: Page 42 at C 6.

10202 W. Washington Boulevard, Culver City.

MONOGRAM STUDIOS

4401 Sunset Boulevard, Los Angeles.

This studio was one of the "Big Three of Poverty Row" along with Republic Studios and PRC (Producers Releasing Corporation).

In my opinion, Republic productions were unquestionably the best in quality, followed by PRC, which leaves Monogram at the bottom of the barrel. But during the Golden Days of Hollywood films, it was a mainstay of neighborhood movie houses - because of quantity rather than quality. Monogram produced more than 700 feature films; the most popular were the BOWERY BOYS and CHARLIE CHAN series.

The studio's location is behind the KCET television studio at 4401 Sunset Boulevard, east of Vermont Avenue, Los Angeles.

Thomas Bros. Map reference: Page 35 at A 3.

The Bronson Gate as seen in SUNSET BOULEVARD (1950).

PARAMOUNT STUDIOS

The Bronson Gate today.

In a clever bit of advertising, Paramount executives filmed scenes for many of their motion pictures at or near the studio entrance. The ornate arch and gates became familiar to moviegoers worldwide in scenes from SUNSET BOULEVARD (1950), HOLLYWOOD OR BUST (1956), the last team appearance of Dean Martin and Jerry Lewis, and the Jerry Lewis comedy THE ERRAND BOY (1961). Elizabeth Taylor fans will remember this location from her television movie THERE MUST BE A PONY (1986).

A much larger entrance was recently constructed west of the original "classic" entrance to provide easier access to the studio complex. Although the new entrance retains the basic architecture of its prototype, the original entrance remains an attraction to thousands of tourists annually.

The main entrance to the studio is located at 5555 Melrose Avenue in Hollywood. The classic entrance is a short distance east, north of the intersection of Melrose Avenue and Bronson Avenue, at the end of Bronson Avenue.

Thomas Bros. Map reference: Page 4 at D 5.

SENNETT STUDIOS

1712 Glendale Boulevard, Los Angeles.　　　　　Close-up of the "Fun Factory".

A unique reminder of the beginning of the "Hollywood" motion picture industry rests on a slope east of Glendale Boulevard at the intersection of Effie Street in Los Angeles.

Once a part of a huge motion picture production complex known as the "Fun Factory", this building now houses a theatre group's scenery and wardrobe.

In years past, the building served as a roller skating rink and a western dance hall.

The building is located at 1712 Glendale Boulevard, north of the Hollywood Freeway (101) in Los Angeles.

Thomas Bros. Map reference: Page 35 at C 5.

HISTORIC MOVIE RANCHES

ARNAZ RANCH (SITE)

On David Avenue looking toward Robertson Boulevard
in Los Angeles.

The Arnaz Ranch, once part of the vast Jose De Arnaz Spanish land grant in the Rincon De Los Bueyes section of Los Angeles, was a spacious area not far from Culver City. The Hal Roach Studios used it for outdoor scenes that called for a "rural" atmosphere. Many short subjects filmed there, including Laurel and Hardy's TOWED IN A HOLE (1932), and Our Gang's SCHOOL'S OUT (1930), THE POOCH (1932) and HELPING GRANDMA (1931).

The site (now a housing tract) is west of Robertson Boulevard, between David Avenue and Beverlywood

IVERSON RANCH

The famous "Indian Head Rock" as seen in
THE AMAZONIANS (1920), TELL IT TO THE MARINES (1925)
and THE PHANTOM EMPIRE (1935).

An opposite view of "Indian Head Rock" as seen in NOAH'S ARK (1928).

Railroad tracks near the ranch entrance seen in many westerns and serials.

The stark but rugged landscape of this historic location, 30 miles from downtown Los Angeles, provided the setting for more than 2,000 motion pictures and movie serials from the 1930s through the 1950s. Virtually every boulder, stagecoach road, trail, gorge, railroad tunnel and twisting highway both on the ranch property and in the immediate area has been filmed countless times for a myriad of motion pictures as well as scores of television series.

"Indian Head Rock" is perhaps the most familiar of the many rock formations scattered throughout the ranch. Near the private ranch house property, "Indian Head Rock" was seen in THE AMAZONIANS and DAVID AND GOLIATH as early as 1920. It was later seen in TELL IT TO THE MARINES (1925), NOAH'S ARK (1928), and the Gene Autry serial THE PHANTOM EMPIRE (1935).

THE CHARGE OF THE LIGHT BRIGADE (1936), Laurel and Hardy's THE FLYING DEUCES (1939), John Wayne's STAGECOACH (1939) and THE FIGHTING SEABEES (1944), FRONTIER PONY EXPRESS (1939),

Henry Fonda's THE GRAPES OF WRATH (1940), WAGON WHEELS WESTWARD (1945) and Gene Autry's HILLS OF UTAH (1951) are only a few of the many motion picture features filmed in other areas of the ranch.

Of interest to Laurel and Hardy fans, the scene from THE FLYING DEUCES filmed at the ranch was the now-famous "laundry" segment. Stan and Ollie, French Foreign Legionnaires assigned laundry duty, tire of washing and ironing tons of clothes and stomp off the job

The tunnel under Santa Susana Pass Road, west of Topanga Canyon Boulevard, seen in many westerns.

The "private" entrance to ranch property.

The famous "Arch Rock" near the private entrance as seen in many segments of THE LONE RANGER television series.

MARVEL (both released in 1941) were filmed at the ranch. And segments of television's THE BIG VALLEY, GUNSMOKE, HAVE GUN - WILL TRAVEL, THE LONE RANGER, THE RIFLEMAN and WAGON TRAIN were also filmed there.

The original entrance to the ranch was Iverson Lane (a private road not to be confused with nearby Iverson Road) that intersected Santa

to tell the Commandant (Charles Middleton) they have decided to resign. In their haste, they accidentally overturn a stove and set the laundry afire.

Serial fans will be delighted to learn that THE PHANTOM EMPIRE, TERRY AND THE PIRATES (1940), DICK TRACY VS. CRIME, INC. and the ADVENTURES OF CAPTAIN

Iverson's stagecoach trail.

Susanna Pass Road exactly 9/10 of a mile from Topanga Canyon Boulevard in Chatsworth. However, a subsequent visit revealed heavy earth-moving equipment swarming about the ranch property, cutting roads and grading areas for the construction of town-houses. A spokesman for the contractor claims that the basic landscape of the ranch as well as the famous rock formations will be left intact as much as

The location of the famous "laundry" scene in Laurel and Hardy's comedy classic THE FLYING DEUCES.

Twisting Santa Susana Pass Road, famous for the chase scenes seen in many serials.

possible for historic reasons. Thus when construction is completed, a visitor to the area will be able to enjoy this important piece of motion picture history by driving the roads or walking the paths and sidewalks to various film locations.

Thomas Bros. Map reference: Page 6 at B 1.

Gene Autry and Champion at Melody Ranch.

MELODY RANCH

In movies from the 1930s through the 1950s, Gene Autry rode the streets and trails of his privately owned ranch. Melody Ranch, although now surrounded by modern homes, looks much as it did during the Golden Age of movie Westerns.

The entrance to Melody Ranch.

The store.

The ranch is on Oak Creek Avenue at Placeritos Boulevard, north of Placerita Canyon Road, west of the Antelope Freeway (14) in Newhall.

Thomas Bros. Map reference: Page 127 at E 3.

The town hall.

Main Street.

AFTERWORD

And so the journey ends.

You have just concluded a make-believe excursion to many "Hollywood" locations dear to moviegoers and television viewers worldwide.

To the reader far away: I hope that this book will encourage you to pursue your dream of a pilgrimage to Hollywood.

To the reader who lives in Southern California:

I hope that you will spend many happy hours exploring and enjoying some or all of these sites.

To all readers: The charm of make-believe Hollywood is eternal. Locations away from the studio retain a tinge of nostalgic magic - after a few months and even after a few decades.

If you doubt this, stand where the famous of motion pictures and television have stood. And be convinced.